The Maoris of New Zealand

The Maoris arrived in New Zealand about 1,200 years ago. They travelled by canoe across the Pacific Ocean. For nearly 1,000 years they lived without being bothered by other people. The arrival of Europeans in the eighteenth century brought struggles over land which ended in war. Since then things have improved. Today, white New Zealanders and Maoris live peacefully together. There are still problems but the Maoris hope for a happy future.

PEOPLE OF THE WORLD

MAORIS

Hilary Lee-Corbin

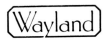

People of the World

Aborigines
Inuit
Kalahari Bushmen
Maoris
Plains Indians
Zulus

All words in **bold** are explained in the glossary on page 46.

Cover: Celebrating a Maori festival at Nqanunawahia.
Frontispiece: Hundreds of visitors have turned up to see Maoris celebrate on a *marae*.

This book is based on an original text by Graham Wiremu

First published in 1989 by
Wayland (Publishers) Ltd
61 Western Road, Hove
East Sussex BN3 1JD, England

© Copyright 1989 Wayland (Publishers) Ltd

Edited by Joan Walters
Consultant: Roger Howarth

British Library Cataloguing in Publication Data
Lee – Corbin, Hilary
    Maoris. – (People of the world).
    1. New Zealand. Maori civilization – for children
    I. Title   II. Series

ISBN 1–85210–825–8

Typeset by Kalligraphics Limited, Horley, Surrey
Printed in Italy by G. Canale and C.S.p.A., Turin
Bound in France by AGM

Contents

The people of New Zealand 6

Chapter 1   A journey over the ocean 8
Who are the Maoris? 8
A new land 10

Chapter 2   How the Maoris lived 12
A new way of life 12
Maori beliefs 14
The Maoris in peace 16
The Maoris at war 18
Maori arts 20
Carving and weaving 22

Chapter 3   The coming of Pakehas 24
The settlers 24
Part of the British Empire 26
The land wars 28
A 'dying race' 30

Chapter 4   The Maoris today 32
Into the twentieth century 32
Maoris in modern New Zealand 34
The Maoris protest 36

Chapter 5   Maori rebirth 38
The Maori way of life 38
The marae 40
The Maori language 42
The Maoris in the future 44

Glossary 46
Index 48

The people of New Zealand

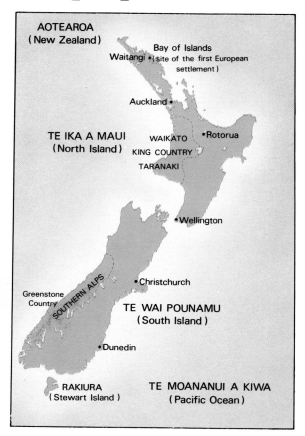

This is a map of New Zealand. It is made up of two large islands and a number of smaller ones. It is in the far south in the Pacific Ocean. In the nineteenth century thousands of people went there to live. They were mainly from Britain.

Before these settlers arrived, another group of people were already living in New Zealand. They were called Maoris. This is the head of a Maori weapon called a **taiaha**.

Here we see a Maori chief of long ago speaking to his people in the middle of a Maori village. Today Maoris speak English, wear the same kinds of clothes and live in the same kinds of houses as other New Zealanders. This book tells about how the Maoris lived before the settlers came and how they fought for their land and freedom.

Chapter 1   A journey over the ocean

Who are the Maoris?

Until about 1,000 years ago there were no humans living in New Zealand. The first people came by canoe from the **tropical** islands in the Pacific Ocean. In this map we can see how far they travelled.

➡

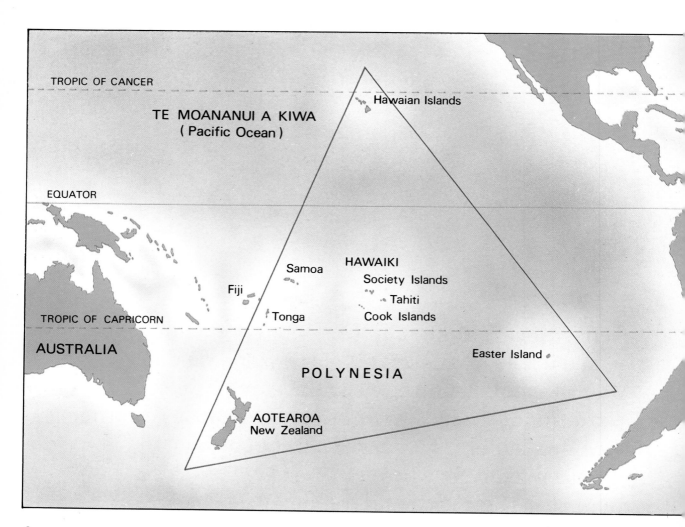

The boats the Maoris sailed in were made from two canoes tied together. The Maoris are related to the Polynesians who live on the islands of Tahiti, Cook, Hawaii and Easter Island. We know this because their languages are similar and because they look alike. Also their **myths** and **legends** are similar. In this picture we can see what many of the sailing boats they travelled in were like.

A new land

The Polynesians set out in their canoes, leaving their tropical homes for ever. Here is a picture of a Pacific island like those they left behind them.

➤

New Zealand came as a shock to these first men and women. It was a lot colder than the lands they had left. Many of the plants they had brought with them ▸ would not grow. Also the land was much bigger and wilder than anything they had seen before.

They found a strange bird living in their new land. It was called a **moa**. ◀ Some were taller than men. Sadly they were hunted so much that they became extinct.

11

Chapter 2   How the Maoris lived

A new way of life

Families began to settle down in their new land and to build villages. A family belonged to a **hapu**, or part of a tribe, and several parts made up a tribe or **iwi**. The tribe owned all the land. It did not belong to one particular person.

The **kumara** is like a small knobbly potato but sweeter. The Maoris brought it with them from their homeland and it became an important part of their food in New Zealand. In this picture we see women preparing and cooking *kumara*.

Every tribe had its chief. A chief or **rangatira** might have more than one wife and often several slaves as well. These were usually prisoners captured from other tribes. Here we see a *rangatira* and his wife dressed in beautiful clothes.

Maori beliefs

Maoris had their own religion. Part of their religious beliefs was that certain people, places or objects were **sacred** or forbidden. This belief was called **tapu**.

The bones of the dead were also *tapu*. They were cleaned and ▶ painted and kept in a carved box like this.

◀ In this picture we see an old **tohunga** or wise man. He is in a *tapu* state and must not touch cooked food, so he is being fed by a boy.

The amount of land the Maoris owned increased their **mana** or honour. This was very important to the Maoris. It could be shared by the whole tribe and was worth dying for. If someone hurt another person's *mana* or broke a *tapu*, the Maoris believed terrible things would happen. The chief, or *tohunga*, punished anyone who went against *mana* or *tapu*.

The Maoris in peace

What was it like to live in a Maori **kainga** or village hundreds of years ago? In the forests there were birds and plants to eat and the rivers were full of fish, so there was plenty of food. The women wove cloth to make clothes and children were taught by the elders. But there was plenty of time to play. Here we see Maoris on a huge swing.

➡

Sometimes people from another tribe would visit and
there would be feasting, singing and dancing in the
marae or central open space of the *kainga*. Maoris
enjoyed themselves in other ways too. They flew
kites or spun tops. In the evening they gathered in
their huts to sing songs and tell stories.

The Maoris at war

Boys learned to fight from an early age and most grew up to be very strong. They used several weapons. The *taiaha* was a spear made of wood. There were clubs made of whalebone, wood and a kind of jade called greenstone. This greenstone club was called the **patu pounamu** and was supposed to be the most dangerous. Maoris did not use bows and arrows. These Maori warriors are doing a **peruperu**, or war dance.

➡

Wars were usually fought for land, but the *mana* of
the tribe also had to be guarded against insults. In
this picture we see a Maori fortress, called a **pa.** This
pa was built on an island, making attacks from
enemies as difficult as possible. Sometimes wars
were ended by marriages between members of the
fighting tribes. They would give each other presents
and hope for a peaceful life.

Maori arts

This is the inside of a Maori meeting house which
has been beautifully carved. A lot of Maori art is
found only in New Zealand and not in the islands of
Polynesia. When the Maoris got to New Zealand
they found new materials to work with. They were
then able to make new designs and to find ways of
working which were all their own.

Carving was done by men and weaving by women.
These skills were often used together in the
decorations as in the picture below.

Carving and weaving

Using only stone tools, the Maori men made very
beautiful wood carvings with swirling spirals and
wriggling monsters. The *pa* or fortress had carvings
of monsters to frighten away enemies. The Maoris
even carved themselves. This was called tattooing.
They carved patterns into their skin with tiny
chisels. This is a portrait of a Maori chief with
tattoos on his face.

⬆

The women wove from different types of **flax** and other plants which grow in New Zealand. They did not have **looms** so work was slow. In the picture above, we see women weaving cloaks. They also made baskets, floor mats, sandals and simple clothes. The cloth they made was often decorated with zig-zag patterns.

Chapter 3   The coming of Pakehas

The settlers

The Maoris had to **adapt** their way of life when they settled in **Aotearoa** as they called New Zealand. The greatest challenge of all was when the Europeans arrived. They called them **Pakehas**. When Captain James Cook arrived in 1769 they began to see more white men. In this picture, painted by an English sailor, we see a Maori and a European giving each other a present.

Although *Pakehas* brought new ideas and
materials ike iron, cloth and pottery and also new
animals and crops, they brought bad things too.
Diseases which the Maoris had never had were
brought by Europeans. The chiefs in the picture
above were taken to England by a **missionary**. One
returned to New Zealand with guns to kill his
enemies. Missionaries taught the Maoris how to
read and write but the Maoris did not become
Christian at once.

Part of the British Empire

In 1840 a law was made which protected the Maoris. It was called the Treaty of Waitangi. In return the Maoris agreed to become British subjects. When people first arrived from Britain to settle in New Zealand, they were able to buy land from the Maoris for almost nothing. The Maoris did not understand that the settlers wanted the land for themselves for ever. Many battles were fought because of this. Here we see a chief talking to his warriors before setting off for war.

After the Treaty of Waitangi New Zealand became
part of the British Empire. The *Pakehas* were not all
bad. Some taught the Maoris new ways of farming
as we can see in the picture above. But the British
still took Maori land and more fighting broke out
in the 1840s.

The land wars

By 1860 there were more *Pakeha* settlers than
Maoris. They were taking more and more land.
Some Maori chiefs realized that they would have to
fight for their land. In this picture we see Maoris
fighting *Pakeha* soldiers. Maoris were very good at
fighting in the forests, but they were outnumbered.
The fighting went on until all the Maori leaders
were defeated.

Many British soldiers did not like fighting the Maoris. They thought the wars were unfair. The Maoris stood very little chance of winning because the British had more men and more guns. Not only did many Maoris lose their lives in the fighting but they lost a lot of their land and their *mana*. These Maori prisoners of war are being guarded on a prison ship in Wellington harbour.

A 'dying race'

The time after the wars of the 1860s and 1870s was very bad for the Maori people. They continued to lose land because of new laws. Even if they still had their farms, they could not borrow money to spend on them like the *Pakehas*. It was thought that they were a 'dying race' and would soon disappear altogether. Happily, this did not happen.

Some Maori people wanted to be left alone. This is a picture of King Tawhiao, who took his people away to land now known as the King Country, where they were not bothered by the *Pakehas*.

We can see how poor and unhappy the Maoris look
in this picture. It was taken in the King country.
Instead of fighting the world of the *Pakehas*, slowly
they became part of it. They made sure though that
they kept their old ways and beliefs.

Chapter 4   The Maoris today

Into the twentieth century

During this **century** Maori chiefs encouraged their people to learn the skills of the *Pakehas* but at the same time to keep their old ways of living. One such leader was Sir Apirana Ngata, who can be seen in the picture below. Slowly the Maori people began to take their place in the government of New Zealand.

Maori men fought in both world wars. This is a picture of Maori troops during the Second World War. They were very good fighters. The Second World War meant big changes for those who stayed at home too. Many people were needed to work in factories. This meant that Maoris began to leave their homes in the country to live in the towns and cities.

Maoris in modern New Zealand

Most of the Maoris today live in the towns and cities and have the same sort of life as the *Pakehas*. On the whole, all people in New Zealand live happily together.

Some Maori people have become famous, for example Kiri Te Kanawa, the opera singer. Here we see the All Blacks rugby team in action. Many of the players are Maoris.

Visitors to New Zealand are usually impressed by
what they see of Maori life. In this picture a girl in
Maori costume stands by a carved gateway.

The Maoris protest

The loss of so much of their land still makes many Maoris angry. Recently there have been several protests. This is the Maori Land March which took place in 1975.

Here Maoris occupied land which they believed to be theirs. The land was sold and they felt very unhappy about it.

Not all Maoris have such pleasant lives as *Pakehas*. They often live in poorer houses, have poorer education and health care and they do the jobs that no one else wants. Today Maoris are fighting back. They want to be thought of as the equals of the *Pakehas*. They want the Maori way of life, their language and their customs to be respected.

Chapter 5   Maori rebirth

The Maori way of life

Maoris realize how many of their old ways of doing things have already been lost. They want to hang on to what is left. Because of this, many people have become interested in the Maori way of doing things. This is called **Maoritanga.**

Today many Maoris, who were brought up to speak only English, are learning their old language. The old arts of weaving, carving, singing, dancing and story-telling are also being taught. These Maori women are learning to weave.

➡

The traditional Maori greeting of rubbing noses is called **hongi.** Many Maoris would rather live the old Maori way and keep their traditions alive.

The marae

On page 17 we saw how visitors from one tribe were welcomed to the *marae*, or open space, in the village. Here is a present day warrior challenging visitors arriving at his *marae*.

↑

These Maoris are at a **hui**. A *hui* may be a wedding, a meeting or sometimes a **tangi**. A *tangi* is a Maori funeral. At a *hui* there will usually be speeches, singing and dancing. It will also be a time for meeting old friends, making new ones and sharing food cooked in the old ways.

The Maori language

The Maori elders in this picture are making
speeches in the Maori language. We have seen a
number of Maori words in this book. They may look
strange to people who are not Maori. Even some
Maoris have difficulty in saying them properly
because for years their language was forbidden and
they had to learn English.

Slowly, times are changing and now the Maori language is being taught again. Even on television, the news-readers and weather forecasters try to pronounce Maori place names properly. Parents can send their children to a **kohanga reo**. This is a school where children can learn both Maori and English.

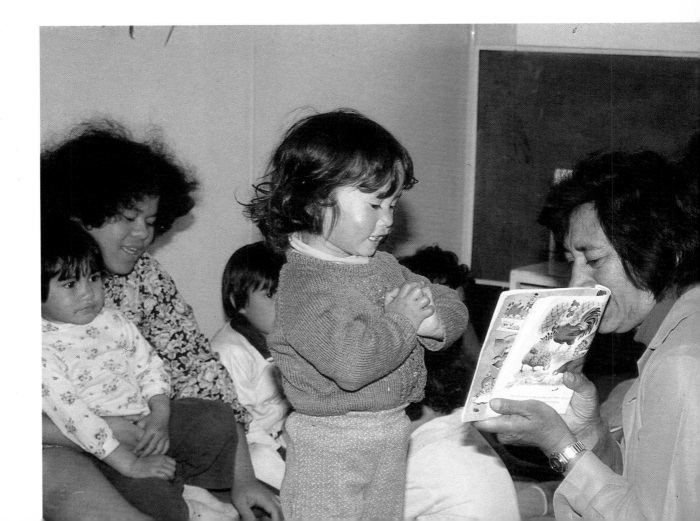

The Maoris in the future

Today the number of Maoris is increasing. A hundred years ago, it was thought that they were dying out. One thing is certain, the Maori people will continue to fight to be equal to *Pakehas*. In this picture we see a famous star, David Bowie, with Maori people watching a ceremony at a *marae*.

➡

In 1984 Maoris marched to protest about the way they have been treated. There have been many such protests and slowly, *Pakehas* are beginning to see that the Maoris are right. They realize that the Maori way of life has a lot to offer New Zealand. Maoris young and old, men and women, are working in their different ways to make New Zealand a better country for Maoris of the future to live in.

Glossary

Adapt   To change in order to survive in different situations and conditions.

Century   A period of time lasting one hundred years.

Extinct   No longer existing. When an animal or plant has died out completely it is said to be extinct.

Flax   A plant grown for the fibres in its stem which can be used to make cloth. The Maoris use flax to weave screens and baskets.

Legends   Popular stories handed down from family to family. After many years nobody remembers whether or not they are true stories.

Loom   A framework on which wool, or other yarns, is woven into cloth.

Missionary   Someone who travels to a foreign country to convert people to a particular religion.

Moa   A very large bird which could not fly. It used to live in New Zealand but has now become extinct.

Myths   Stories about superhuman beings which tell us how certain customs came to be.

Sacred   Highly respected and honoured especially in a religious sense.

Tropical   Situated in the tropics where the weather is hot and damp.

Glossary of Maori words

Aotearoa   The Maori name for New Zealand.

Hapu   Part of a tribe.

Hongi   The traditional Maori greeting of rubbing noses.

Hui   A gathering of people or a celebration.

46

Iwi   A tribe.

Kainga   A Maori village.

Kohanga reo   A nursery school where children go to learn the Maori language.

Kumara   A small, sweet potato.

Mana   The Maori sense of honour and prestige.

Maoritanga   The Maori way of life.

Marae   Open space and community centre within a Maori village.

Pa   A Maori fortress.

Pakeha   A European or a person who is not Maori.

Patu pounamu   A greenstone club, considered the most precious of weapons.

Peruperu   A war dance.

Rangatira   A chief in a tribe.

Taiaha   A long weapon with a sharp point at one end and a flat blade at the other.

Tangi   A time of mourning or a funeral.

Tapu   Something which is sacred and forbidden.

Tohunga   A priest or a wise man.

Picture Acknowledgements

The illustrations in this book were supplied by the following:

Alexander Turnbull Library, Wellington 7, 9, 12, 13, 16, 17, 19, 25, 26, 27, 29, 30, 32, 33; Auckland City Art Gallery 15, 22, 23; Auckland Institute and Museum 28; British Library 24; Peter Bush 34; Department of Maori Affairs *frontispiece*, 36, 37, 39, 40, 41, 42, 43, 44, 48; Department of Maori Studies, Victoria University, Wellington 31; National Museum of New Zealand 6 (lower), 11 (lower), 14, 18, 20, 21; National Publicity Studio of New Zealand 10, 11 (upper), 35; Axel Poignant *cover*; Wayland Picture Library 38, 39. Maps on pages 6 and 8 by Bill Donohoe. Picture research by Philip Whaanga.

Index

Animals 25
Arts 20–21
   carving 20, 21, 22, 38
   weaving 16, 20, 21, 23, 38

Birds 11, 16
Britain 6, 26

Canoes 8, 9, 10
Children 16
Clothes 7, 13, 16
Cook, Captain James 24
Cooking 12, 41

Dancing 17, 38, 41
Diseases 25, 30

Education 37
Europeans, see *Pakehas*

Farming 27
Fighting 7, 26, 27, 28
Food 12, 14, 16, 41

Government 30, 32

Health care 37
Hongi 39
Houses 7, 21, 37
Hui 41
Hunting 11

King country 30, 31

Languages 9, 37, 38, 42, 43
Laws 26, 30

Mana 15, 19, 29
Maori land 13, 15, 26, 27, 28, 29,
   30, 36, 37
Maoritanga 38
Marae 17, 40, 44
Marriage 19
Missionaries 25

Pakehas 24, 25, 27, 28, 30, 31, 32,
   34, 37, 44, 45
Peruperu 18
Plants 10, 16, 23
Playing 16, 17

Religion 14

Schools 43
Singing 17, 38, 41
Story-telling 17, 38

Tangi 41
Tapu 14, 15
Tohunga 14, 15
Tribal chiefs 7, 13, 22, 26, 28, 32
Tribes 12, 13, 15, 17

Villages 7, 12, 16

Wars 19, 30, 33
Weapons 6, 18
   guns 25, 29
   patu pounamu 18
   taiaha 6, 18